Inspirations To Help You Find Your Path To Truth

Dr Frances Robinson

Inspirations To Help You Find Your Path To Truth
© Dr Frances Robinson

All rights reserved. No part of this publication may be reproduced, stored in a retrieval system, or transmitted in any form or by any means, electronic, mechanical, photocopying, recording or otherwise, without the prior written permission of the author.

National Library of Australia Cataloguing-in-Publication entry

Author:	Robinson, Dr Frances, author.
Title:	Inspirations To Help You Find Your Path To Truth / Dr Frances Robinson
ISBN:	9780992442804 (paperback)
Subjects:	Truth--Religious aspects.
	Inspiration--Religious aspects.

Dewey Number: 121.0882

Published with the assistance of www.loveofbooks.com.au

CONTENTS

1. **The Last Door** — 5
   - Physician heal thyself — 5
   - More on the Last Door — 7

2. **Who am I? What have I studied?** — 10
   - My Hypothesis on the Healing Process — 13
   - Physician heal thyself — 14

3. **The purpose of this book** — 16
   - Stages of Healing — 19
   - Humility and Love — 19
   - Forgiveness and Love — 20
   - Self-Respect — 21
   - Laughter and Happiness — 22
   - Inner Light/Peace — 22
   - Appreciation – "to life" — 23

4. **The Seven Step Plan** — 26
   - 'Transformation of the Self' — 26
   - Mind over matter, our thoughts do count — 28
   - They say "old soul, new soul" — 28

5. **The Chakra's** — 30
   - Mediation to Transform your Thought Patterns — 31
   - Action and Reaction — 32
   - The Chakra System — 32

Step 1 – Root Base Chakra	34
Step 2 – The Sacral Chakra: Pelvic	35
Step 3 – The Solar Plexus Chakra	35
Step 4 – The Heart Chakra: Love	37
Step 5 – The Throat Chakra	38
The Mind Chakra, The Third Eye	39
The Seventh Chakra	40
The Lost Soul	42
Summary	43
6. The Soul, the Mind and Pain	**45**
Why is suffering necessary?	46
The Mind	46
7. Crying for Reality of Pure Love	**52**

The Last Door

WHEN THE DOOR CLOSES BEHIND YOU,
'LOOK FOR THE LIGHT'.

PHYSICIAN HEAL THYSELF

Do not be shocked or surprised when my life starts with this disclosure – "I have personally witnessed 6,000 souls pass over, as a part of my work + life". My nickname during the 80's to 2000 was Dr. Death and that was an appropriate name because my life involved being near death being involved in death, studying death and helping souls pass over.

My life has always been back to front. People usually live life and learn about death at the end of life – I have done everything back to front in my life. I started life learning about death and as life has gone by without my dying, I have come to start learning about life – always back to front.

"In another life I could fly – In this life I dance"

So, my story starts in a little town...

I was born into poverty and by the age of 4 years I had decided I was an Indian princess stolen at birth and lost to this family and people. I could also naturally see ghosts. I felt guilty about my thought that I belonged to better people and I was afraid of the ghosts. I had to sleep with the light on in my own room in a family of eight in a tiny house. I had my own tiny room. My mother loved me and let me paint it bright pink. I had thought it would bring me happiness. It did not. My father was a commando and had been to war and personally slit the throats of about twelve Japanese young men. He remembered the deaths all the time and drank himself to death. I remembered the ghosts and was terrified of the night. I came to understand later why I was terrified of the night. In my previous birth in Pakistan I had been beaten to death. I came to understand this later in my life because God gave me a vision of the beating. The vision gave me understanding, closure, maturity and an ability to empathize with other people my psychiatric conditions. It gave me more compassion and understanding. I could turn the light off at night and sleep in the comfort that only an awareness of God's love and presence could give.

The love from God as a gift can never be presumed or under appreciated. It is not automatic.

I have a strong longing to tell my story as I feel it is a part of my journey in myself healing. I believe telling my story maybe of interest to others because my life has been enormously busy, eventful and full of learning – I have always wanted to teach and never had a chance and if anyone finds this book an aid to learning I will have filled another lifelong desire. Finally, I have a hypothesis to share on the steps of healing the spirit. The inspiration for this book comes from 3 huge influences of my life.

1) Dr Elizabeth KublerRoss
2) Dr Scott Peck
3) Dr Christine Page "Frontiers of health"

I felt she (a doctor like me) can write openly about what is obvious to me and get accepted (not defamed and humiliated) then she has opened the door for likeminded people to also take that chance and share their experiences.

MORE ON THE LAST DOOR

Like Dr Peck I have seen many, many cases and examples that form a pattern that must mean something. Presently I am dealing with a difficult case who is approaching "the last door". Everyone in this life has so many chances at life. So many chances to get it right and so many opportunities to heal. What about when it becomes unfair on the entire human race, on earth and the world. That's when people start to 'cheat' and want more than their fair share.

"What goes around comes around"

What about when someone has had every possible chance on Earth and uses it and wastes it all. This happens. These people have such a "chip on their shoulder" that they are saved that they take and take and never give a drop back. They clearly push so fair to see how far they can push. My only hope for them as I'm standing in a lighted democracy is that they wake up to themselves before it's too late, before time runs out. The light starts to dim and finally the door is closed.

I mean of course "the last door"

There are no more doors, only more of the same and darkness. Finally they are left in the dark screaming their rights of fairness and justice. Screaming to no one, alone, afraid, and with no answer. The last door closed naturally when time and all good intentions and good will were finally run out and finished. Dr Scott Peck I think would have called that sad. I would call that a kind of Purgatory for that particular soul.

Lost, alone, in the dark and the last door has closed.

Back to my life and my influences before I form my hypothesis. After being born into poverty and a father who was insane, he taught me about PTSS. He taught me about compassion and I watched the man die slowly and painfully. I observed the body slowly die around a defeated and tortured soul. I sat with him with a bucket while he bled for three hours while waiting for an ambulance and I thought "I can do better than this, I'm going to become a doctor". At the same time this happened a young beautiful friend of mine was hit by a car. Mindless act of cruelty. She lay bleeding and dying on the road for three hours and the ambulance didn't arrive before she died. A very cruel soul came to me to describe her death and as he did I felt her soul visit me and I felt myself promising in anyway possible to dedicate my life to stopping such events (life changing events).

All my life is about choices, same time I read the book "pathways" changed my life. Each choice each step is a pathway. A direction to the future. A light. This life of mine has been a long journey with God pointing me in the directions and pathways I must take. Which brings me back to the chapter of this book "The Last Door". Through my own learning and experiences of this life and with my spiritual training and medical training I have been brought to the belief that for many people I have become "The Last Door". What I exactly mean by that is at some point (not by chance) they have been brought to me to make a last choice, a last decision, with the aid of spiritual light. They are in the position of having to make a pathway choice. For reason that are clear to me, for these people it is their 'last door'. Once their choice is made, their door is closed and their own decision is final. Ceiling their future destiny. Just as my life has been set out before me and I will continue to describe how, I still believe it is predetermined destiny that must be filled with impels me to write this book, this story, so my soul can be at peace with itself and the world.

Who am I?
What have I studied?

I am approaching sixty, I grew up in poverty and got a scholarship to Monash University medical school. I loved medicine, I loved to study and got high distinctions and honours. I had fun and loved Monty Python. I loved microbiology and the study of infectious diseases, I didn't know I was spiritual while I was studying. I was also very depressed despite my joy of study. One night I went to the top of the building like so many other students and stood for hours looking at the jump to suicide. Not emotional, I remember contemplating... "to jump or not to jump, that is the question"

At midnight I got tired and went to bed. I only did that once. I did not seek help or treatment as many did not back then, I just kept studying. After graduation I was an intern at the Alfred Hospital in Melbourne. This was the hardest year old my life. Many flashbacks come from that first year, one hundreds hours a week. I was sleep deprived, there were at least five deaths a week, all of them were traumatic. Many bad memories and yet this year there were so many choices. Exhaustion, tiredness, to help people or not to? To care or not to care? To become closed and empty or fight to keep spiritually alive? Many of my stories of work come from the six years of junior doctor I did. I learnt, I become clever, good at work "top gun" hard and arrogant.

Almost suddenly, I realized I was depressed, my life lacked love. Very suddenly and definitely god found me and made me his own and filled my life with the love that was missing. He found me, he said you belong to me and he made me his own. I went to India to an ashram to meditate on love and God. Details aren't too necessary when they've now made a movie called "eat, pray, love". When I saw it I thought gee, I did that twenty years ago. Now it's become famous. Suffice to say I did it, then whammo, huge MVA and I'm in a coma in the Alfred Hospital. Multiple broken bones, death experience. Going to the light, come back etc. Details are so boring. Yet the MVA and the following six months illness destroyed my ego. I discovered humility, God again, compassion, empathy, a feeling for every hurt and injured person everywhere. All hardness and ego dissolved in love, kindness, and understanding. It is obvious that destiny and God worked together. Planned the whole thing for my greater learning and to chance who I was as a doctor. After I had recovered from the accident I was overwhelmed with compassion and empathy and felt a huge something missing in myself. I walked past the palliative care ward and saw the eyes of the patients. Eyes without hope light or love and filled with fear. I joined the palliative care ward where I worked for ten years and finally incorporated oncology into my learning curve. Now at this point it is very important to say one of the very most important things I observed. Everyone is at first afraid of their own mentality and death including health professionals. It is at six months work the crunch comes. The professional is faced with their own mortality, choices and pathways. They must choice to face their mortality.

   1) Learn to learn and grow
      Or
   2) Shut down, close out the fear

Eg. Change jobs or become deadly closed to the emotional stats of patients, I call it "dead face".

This is one of the most important things I learnt due to its repercussions to the health professional world. Then you see weird things from there that it's best not to discuss in front of the very innocent trusting public. The bible for all workers in this field is Dr Elizabeth Kubler Ross. I read all her books more than once and cried through every world. What master of compassion and help for patients. The woman is now recognized for her world. I worked two years at mount Ohvelt hospital and learnt so much, another books worth.

Then it was time to move on. Dying and hospital work taught me a new way to learn, through humor and happiness. "Laughter is the best medicine". I worked with a very good friend with an enormous sense of humor, a great doctor, worshipped by his patients and he died. He taught me a new view of humor. One of the nicest, most wonderful men with the best sense of humor, all in a palliative care ward while he knew he was dying! Humor is so important in medicine. Laughter is the best medicine.

You maybe dying by you can still laugh. He knew he was dying but he had no fear and no regrets which is important. After this work eventually I have ended up in general practice for twelve years. I am now learning about life and people and a different sort of laughter and humor. I cannot stress enough, laughter is still the best medicine and no amount of pills can replace that. This is where I have to come to learn all my knowledge of life, medicine, people's emotions, love and humanity. All this time I have also been studying spirituality, its appreciation to the health professional and the healing process. Do we just go alternate, throw away all our drugs and refer to a naturopath? No, we keep science, we keep our drugs, we keep our alternate therapists and we all work together.

This is who I am. This is what I've studied. This is what I believe. Next I will explain my beliefs on the process of healing. For all the cynics out there and the ones who know me, what hope of all working together in peace?

MY HYPOTHESIS ON THE HEALING PROCESS

The grief process as described by Dr Elizabeth Kubler Ross is easy to follow, easy to understand, reproducible. You can watch thousands of people with the diagnosis of cancer orderly march into the stages of grief as predicted and as expected. Are we not more deeper thinking, conscious beings? At times I think not. But no, we are spiritual, conscious beings with awareness that can take to a higher level. Therefore I hypothesize if we can easily go through stages of grief and loss ?????????. If we can go through the stages of healing, maybe not so easily or precisely. Maybe takes more spiritual efforts, perseverance to go through the stages of healing. But if you knew it was possible, wouldn't you want to try? I will attempt in the following chapters to go through the stages of healing as I have proposed and then address the issues that may be obstacles.

PHYSICIAN HEAL THYSELF

We must all accept that life at this time is actually a learning curve, a destiny of learning. Anyone that says they have nothing to learn, they have learnt it all is in complete denial. Denial is the first stage of grief. I am writing this piece keeping in mind that I wish to hypothesize the understanding of the well accepted theories of stages of grief with some new theories on the stages of grief or places of healing. Understand that life's lesson on healing take the entire life and some more. Therefore the stages of healing spiritually can take the entire life. We understand when we heal a wound, there are stages of physical healing. I tell patients this type of healing may take one week, three months or a year depending on the type of healing. What about emotional, mental and spiritual healing. Depending on the disease or the problem it may take a year, several years, a lifetime or more. To me, this is a really important subject and more communication should occur on this subject. For example, I just met a woman for healing on the subject of her breast cancer.

Healing
 1) The physical wound is healed
 2) The adjuvant therapy chemo/radiotherapy completed. The wound looks good.

Healing phase two. The woman is investigating the causes of her cancer (refer to the book "frontiers on health") the lady had stress, anxiety, lack of nurturing, anger, bitterness and a deep wound to the heart. Which she recognizes are the cause of cancer.

Phase two. Recognizing the spiritual cause corresponding the physical disease. With this recognition comes some "shock+horror". Disappointment with the journey of her life bring her to this point. Sadness with the lack of love and support in her life. Anger at the causes, confusion regarding the direction of her life and future and clearly, a lack of understanding in the next steps needed in her healing process.

The Purpose of this Book

To define the connection between physical disease and the spiritual lessons to be learnt + the steps in the path of healing.

This is the purpose of the book, together I hope we can make some steps forward. In the past what would happen to this woman, this patient (not this spiritual entity on journey of life's learning). She would be referred for counselling by a psychologist (someone I feel has a degree to know nothing, I said that in a fit of delirium and will deny saying this in court, I had a fever). She will be told she is not to blame. She will be asked to gather as much family support as possible to help her through the disease. She will be told she will be supported while she recovers.

I am a GP and also quite spiritual and I believe most of this counselling may be comforting by may also be so far from the truth. Cancer of the breast is connected with spiritual nurturing disease. Long and complicated causes but often close family members and loved ones are actually connected with the initiation of the disease. These are the same ones we are asking to be the support during the healing process? Let me digress (go backwards). During my many years in the cancer unit I would sometimes have very clear Psychic experiences that would shock me. The patient would be nicely and safely tucked up in their bed. We are looked after them and a visitor would arrive in visiting hours who quite clearly in my psychic mind was the cause of their cancer. Obviously their condition would deteriorate during the visit. This other karmic connection was actually the cause of their disease and would be visiting regularly to make sure the job was done! (i.e. They would die). These experiences in my life have certainly changed my vision and outlook on the world from fully physical to destiny a world that is directed by the spiritual, the mind and the emotions. These things are not measured by a CT scan or a blood test. These things are what we really dumb people are called 'subtle' influences on health by they are not subtle.

These are the accepted phases of grief
1) Denial
2) Anger
3) Bargaining (compromise)
4) Depression
5) Acceptance – with attachment – accepting reality, although full of grief

It is called natural. This is my hypothesis of the phase of healing for your consideration.

1) "physical heal thyself"

Instead of denial, have an acceptance of a different reality. A bigger picture. A changed consciousness, an altered awareness.

2) Not anger but self-love

Love for the world and everything. As the Beaties said, Love, Love, Love. Not anger, but forgiveness.

3) An attitude to the world

Instead of bargaining with the world, again change of attitude and vision. Is everything "as is your vision of the world, so is the reality of your world". View life as your friend, teacher and not your enemy.

4) Grief equals depression

If you have started on the path of healing, then humor and happiness are your friend. I will describe this more later with 'best patient ever'

5) Grief leads to acceptance of loss

And often death, as the end of the line. The finish.

I wish to challenge this concept. Grief and death I challenge are just the beginning part of a long line of choices to be made. I wish to challenge this with out outcomes of hope, light, love and future. These are my spiritual markers of healing verses not healing. Where I should invest my spiritual and medical energy and where I should not. There is only so much one medical worker can do. Measure the progress physically, emotionally, spiritually because (as with all science) out come becomes clear and obvious.

Stages of Healing

'PHYSICIAN HEAL THYSELF,

LET THERE BE LIGHT AND THERE WAS LIGHT'

HUMILITY AND LOVE

Instead of denial, acceptance of a different reality. A changed consciousness, stop blaming others for your misery. We can understand the reality may look very real and convincing and I've heard people go over their stories thousands of times. It took me years to understand point one. It looks like this, it should be the reality. If it was the truth then why haven't you started healing? Each phase of healing takes a virtue and help from God, the light of all lights, love. So the first virtue needed is the humility to look at things differently. My world was created by my choices and I cannot blame anyone for them. My choices probably started before this birth. When I made my contract with God (in the womb) about what I agreed to learn this birth, what things I should go through to spiritually move forward.

Phase 1 – the humility to have a new awareness and consciousness about what my illness is all about and what I am to learn through it. Again, I can hear you screaming back, e.g. using myself as an example, I had a major car crash nearly killing me. Did I ask for the car to crash? Well I did and through it I learned so many lessons.

Major events, major learning. The opposite of learning and humility is self-pity, poor me I had a car accident! Obstacles to phase 1 – It's easier to have self-pity then humility and a changed consciousness. There is so much self-gain through illness that you have to be strict on the self not to take that secondary self-gain. I cannot heal because all the reasons on earth that benefits me being sick. E.g. Victim role, patient role, self-pity role. Surely secondary gain is easy to understand. Fundamental exclusion to phase 1 that needs to be clearly states. The decision has to be made before the healing progress can begin that suicide is not an option, suicide has been excluded as an option. This includes suicide varieties i.e. Suicide by chemo, suicide by treatment and non-co-operation. Lately I've had a tricky patient with suicide by slow death and intent, for all purposes pretending to co-operate. I should have seen through it. I took her vibration of misery and suffering as an indication of illness instead of what it really meant, a very real intent to suicide by whatever means.

FORGIVENESS AND LOVE

Phase 2 – Love all with forgiveness, forgiveness is the highest virtue known to man and the closest to God. Without the power of forgiveness which is directly connected to the power of God's love, no healing can ever take place. The power of forgiveness, many books can be written just on this. It's a great power and is very rare. Do you yet have any inkling of a vision why the power of forgiveness. If you are working in the trade like I am, the answers are all the time – he, she, it, them don't deserve it. I'd rather die than forgive! Then there is your choice, why do you need a doctor? End of this story.

Forgiveness step 2 – I didn't say healing was easier than grief, I said it was just as natural and follows a basic set of rules. Judgment is reserved for God, forgiveness is available to all.

SELF-RESPECT

Step 3- Accepted your life, accepted your reality, accepted your situation and forgiveness occurred. (Tears occurred). Now accept yourself as a worthwhile member of society, family and humility. Accept yourself as an important member of God's family. Start to believe in yourself and have self-respect. When you accept yourself the outcomes are joy, laughter, happiness, and a sense of humor you didn't know you had. Leave the darkness behind.

Stage 4 – Humor, happiness are your friends, best patient ever. The healing path is not for the faint of heart. This phase is a crucial phase. The patient needs to step back, become detached from 'who I am'. Have a good look at themselves from a distance, and have a good hearty laugh at themselves. At their situation, a laugh at who they are, what they have become, what healing they need. Laughter is the best medicare, learn to laugh at yourself! The best patient ever is the patient who has learnt to laugh. Ok. I take you take in time. When did all this theory of healing start? I kid you not, it started with Monty Python in the 1980's. Their contribution to the art of healing I don't believe has been recognized. The most famous song is needed now, always look on the bright side of life and death. The song is from Life of Brian, a satire on the life of Jesus Christ. "When life is jolly rotten, there's something you've forgotten, and that's to smile and laugh and dance and sing!"

LAUGHTER AND HAPPINESS

Stage 4 – Stand back and have a good laugh at yourself.

INNER LIGHT/PEACE

Stage 5 – Death can be just the beginning, 'The Challenge'

The final stages of healing are visible as inner peace, 'a light, a lightness, the solar spirit'. As karma is cleared and lifted, the light of a new day comes. The light of a new beginning, something has ended, something has healed. The light of the healing gives a new energy, a new life's purpose. A spiritual investment, that something new can begin. The

positive energy can be invested in a new positive experience, a new learning or a new beginning. Its spiritual money in the spiritual bank that can be invested wisely. Outcomes of positive healing can be measured and seen. Such as visible signs of healing:
- New hope in the future
- New light surrounding the person, soul or spirit
- New or reawakened love for life, nature, family, community, relationships or people. A changed attitude, a positive attitude.
- Life is good (movie life is beautiful), life is worthwhile, valuable, should be cherished and valued

The natural consequence, follow on from life is good, is the expectation of the child. Life is good, what will happen next? What will the future bring? Healing leaves the soul or spirit with an attractive childlike trust and innocence that expects the future to be another surprise birthday party!

APPRECIATION – "TO LIFE"

Stage 6 – Gratitude for the healing, thank you

Appreciation for the healing, for life and for the spirit. Deep down the soul knows it has received a gift of healing and totally experiences from the heart a deep heart felt sense of appreciation. This is even if the soul has worked extremely hard for their own healing, that they did a ton of work for their healing. Deep down in their heart they know they could not of done it all alone with no help, that somewhere, somehow, there is something I will call 'spirit' that gave them a little nudge. A little help at the hardest of times and kept them on the correct direction of healing. The spirit was magically just there, just knew when to help. That's magic, the soul want to say thank you but to where and whom? It's such a beautiful thing, the spirit feels so much love back and also feels it is such a beautiful thing. To see a soul healed and made whole again. It is all worthwhile.

Phase 4 – Humor and Happiness; People will start to recognize you as the best patient ever.

Phase 5 – Inner peace, Light; A new day has dawned on your life, a new beginning.

Phase 6 – Gratitude and Appreciation.

In summary, the process of healing includes these steps.

Phase 1 – Acceptance, a changed consciousness, a new reality, free of the misery of blame, full of the virtue of humility.

Phase 2 – Loving all with the power of forgiveness including the self.

Phase 3 – Self-respect, self-love, self-value. You will experience happiness, laughter, joy.

You will have noticed by now I am not measuring outcomes by physical healing. I have seen with my own eyes patients die full of light and love, surrounded by love and peace and God's light. I know fully that they are healed through the process of their illness, they have gone through the stages and are even experiencing their reward for their effort as they pass. Which brings me to the end of what I wanted to say. This is what I have learned this life, this is what I know every soul can achieve in this life if they want to. Healing.

The Seven Step Plan

'Transformation of the Self'

Dear listeners and to those interested. I have been working and studying people now for 30 years. I have been fortunate to be in a position to study the spirit, the soul and its relationship with the physical body very closely due to my work and my very fortunate experiences of the spirit or soul that have bestowed upon me as a blessing. Call it a blessing or call it a gift, it has been bestowed upon me purely so I can help people. I understand this to be a blessing and a gift and I also understand people can accept the advice and help or they can reject it and turn away.

As all people know one of the most powerful gifts God the father has given to us souls is the power of free choice. All souls have the free choice of seeing and following the truth (I like to say the light) to help themselves or they can deny it all, deny that anyone tried to help them, live a lie, blame others and stay in darkness. It is always a free choice.

After 30 years of working I am still surprised every day at peoples choices. Clearly I am not God and will remain in this state of surprise at the behavior of my brothers souls. At times I am so surprised I wonder if I am stupid and ignorant and will never learn. If I look clearly from God's point of view as he smiles at me. I realize I was never meant to know it all or understand it all. That's his job as the father of all souls. He gave me the job of medical doctor to learn to help my brother souls which I have done to the best of my ability. As I feel the times approaching I wish to share with my peers. Due to my love of healing, my love of science and the love of my fellow souls. I have observed a lot about how the souls or spirit works through the physical body. I have also learnt why some can be healed and why some choose never to be healed. We all know the many advantages of being sick, large and small advantages. I know many will be interested in what I have to say, for many things will ring true and for some they will have called me extreme. WHATEVER! I feel the need to write down the truth.

When I was a young woman I studied the teachings of the Raja yoga which teaches that the spiritual soul resides in the body in the forehead and from this position the soul is like a sparkling star. The spirit or soul drives the body just as if it were driving a car. Such a simplified version of anatomy, but the beauty of spiritual study is that it makes perfect sense. The soul is spiritual energy or power and it radiates power, thought and energy to drive the main nerve plexus's like the brain, the spinal centers in the midbrain, and the nervous system behind the heart, the solar plexus system and the lower plexus's. Serving kidneys, fertility and lastly the sacral plexus.

THE NERVE PLEXUS' WE STUDY IN ANATOMY CORRESPONDS TO THE 7 CHAKRA'S

The soul or the spirit is like a star sparkling with the energy of power and thought. This energy drives the body. It is very simple really.

MIND OVER MATTER. OUR THOUGHTS DO COUNT.

Everything that happens to us is for a reason and for a purpose. We can learn from everything, even disease. We can learn to make our thoughts positive. We can use mediation as a time to observe our own attitudes, vision and thoughts. We can use meditations a time of self-introspection, to take charge again of our own thoughts, to be master of our own minds. I have met so many people in my life that think meditation is for hippies. When you think about it many people do it naturally when they are relaxed or at peace. It is actually a natural state to use your mind in a positive way. Everybody does it.

THEY SAY "OLD SOUL NEW SOUL"

This implies we are all different and take different numbers or reincarnation. This means older souls have more memories or "baggage" that they carry that interferes with the natural flow of minds energy. The soul carries memories in its subconscious and deep in it's heart. Thirty years of study and experience is hard to explain in a few pages but know I the soul am in a physical body of matter made of the five elements. There is a major connection between the soul (or spirit) and physical matter which causes an exchange of energy in both directions. My thoughts count, the experience I have from those thoughts count. It's a two way flow, action and reaction. All of these interactions are influenced by memories, environment, circumstances, relationships etc.

For us to make our thoughts positive and most now agree that positive thoughts aids in our wellbeing. We must understand more about the two way flow of action and reaction and how to help ourselves move towards positive thoughts. We need to understand that positive thoughts, positive energy, positive attitudes create positive energy and a positive healing process.

The Chakra's

I am trying to get you involved in how the soul and body interact through energy flows to determine our health or ill health. How our thought patterns are influenced than more than what we would like to believe. We would like to believe we are in control of our minds and all our thought but this is very far from the truth. I wish to explain how the human body had energy centers (called chakra's) that correspond to the nervous system of the body. There are 7 chakras as described by alternate medicine theories. I wish to state there is a spiritual significance to the disease pattern caused by imbalances in the chakra's (or nerve centers) I believe the nerve centers of the neurologically recognized, anatomical centers of the human body correspond to the chakra system. I believe that if the chakra is unbalanced, leads to significant disease. I believe this has been recognized by many therapists but poorly dealt with. Stated again – the chakras correspond to nerve centers relaying information from the brain to the various parts of the body via the spinal cord. The body is a wondrous thing and the soul is an amazing wondrous thing.

People who study the chakras also often see auras, colours, and subtle signs of human health and disease. Each chakra is equal to or more important than the next.

EACH CHAKRA IS EQUAL TO OR MORE IMPORTANT THAN THE NEXT. NO ONE CHAKRA IS DOMINATING THE BODIES HEALTH ALL CENTRES ARE IMPORTANT.

MEDIATION TO TRANSFORM YOUR THOUGHT PATTERNS

Thoughts determine if you feel happy or sad, good or bad, peace or anger. The power of thoughts are ever so important. Most assume the brain houses the mind where all thoughts are generated, WRONG.

Things are much more complicated than that. If it were true than our anti-depressant drugs that nullify the chemicals in the brain and make them balanced would cure everybody but they don't do they?

Thoughts are generated from the mind but the mind is influenced by so many things e.g. External to the body such as relationships, environment, money worries, jobs and even wars.

The mind is just as influenced by internal things to do with your own body and that's where mediation can make a difference. Meditation cannot pay your bills, get you're a new job or a new wife but it can change the experiences you the soul are having within your body.

Transforming your thoughts by changing your awareness and understanding is like a miracle, works better than drugs. Doesn't cost you money, you use your own free will power.

You take charge of your thoughts and you decide what to think.

The power of choice is free.

With correct effort you can again achieve peace and contentment even if you are ill. This is the beauty of transforming negative thoughts to positive thoughts.

ACTION AND REACTION

Thoughts are generated to all levels of the body for various reasons. The stimulus for thoughts coming from within yourself comes from all of the seven chakras of the body. The chakra system is really a reflection of the nervous system of the human body and reflects the nerve plexus's. Different stimuli create actions and reactions in the nervous system creating thought patterns. These thought patterns can be helpful and healing or disruptive. So let us explore the mind and the thoughts.

THE CHAKRA SYSTEM

The three base chakras are related to the physical survival of the body. The three higher chakra's are more subtle and to do with the quality of life of the soul in the body. The seventh, the highest chakra is all important and I will leave till last. All seven chakras generate thoughts that can make you happy or sad.

They generate thought processes through the energy exchange of action and reaction at all seven levels. The quality of these thoughts generated at all seven levels determines how you think, feel and the quality of your life.

The Power of Transforming Your Thoughts

THROUGH THE POWER OF REALISATION OF WHAT WENT WRONG IN YOUR THOUGHTS

STEP 1 – THE ROOT BASE CHAKRA

It represents coming into this birth and the contract the soul had made with God for the souls redemption, its learning, its closure of karmic accounts (debts). It represents the souls understanding why it was born to this place, with these people. What it has to learn and how it is to pay back its debts, to all through this birth. People realize the contract with God it made before the birth, the soul sees where it is coming from and where it needs to go to clear its debts. The contract is made with God but something the soul gets here and changes its mind. It might say to God "this is too hard, I did agree but I cannot go through with this, I want to break the contract, I want out of it". This causes a great confusion of thoughts in the soul. Even the desire to escape the contract or deal by suicide. Can you imagine the confusion caused when the soul doesn't know what's causing all the bad thoughts? ANSWER – through meditation, the soul has to come to terms with its heritage. It is here for a reason. I was born to this land, with these people for a reason. My life is not in vain and it is not for nothing, there is a purpose to this birth. I need to look deeper to find the good reasons for this birth. I need to meditate, find the answers and work with effort towards positivity.

STEP 2: THE SACRAL CHAKRA: PELVIC

It represents the physical relationships of the present birth on the lessons these relationships give. This birth at this time with these relationships are special and important and never a waste of time. These relationships at this time will test you, the reward from what you can learn is spiritual and not physical. You can learn the power of judgment and definitely the power of tolerance, obviously this birth was not a waste of time. Show me someone who denies all this and I call them a L-I-A-R or a new soul with no previous births of karma. One or the other. Answer: become humble, learn your lessons.

STEP 3: THE SOLAR PLEXUS CHAKRA:

This has been the challenge of my life so I feel some ego in being able to talk about it. The solar plexus is the nerve center that feels fear and is difficult to pass, it is the last physical controlled center and is very important. Directly connected to the liver, spleen and immunological centres of fighting disease. Fear directly influences everything. To conquer fear is half the battle. To fall to fear leads to excess drugs, alcohol and running from fear. Face your fears. What are you afraid of? This is half the battle. When you can make your fears seem smaller and readily deal able you can move onto bigger issues. Through this centre you can go beyond your own self-centred selfish thoughts and help others. Hence the virtue of this centre is benevolence. Putting others before yourself empowers you with self-respect and self-empowerment. To enable you to put others before yourself despite your feeling you need the power of forgiveness. You need the power to make the past be the past. Over and forgotten, great humility is needed for this. All seems too good to be true but in helping others comes self-empowerment. If you can do these things you will be rewarded with the ability to see things with more subtle vision. You will be able to tolerate the mundane stupidity of life and have a grander vision of life, thoughts and the power. ANSWER: Face your fears with humility or forgiveness.

Once you have passed the lesson of the lower physical chakra's (including fear). You then have to look at the higher chakra's which have to do with the spiritual side of the self and required deep self-contemplation. FOR GOD'S SAKE START WITH FORGIVING YOURSELF.

My experience of dealing with fear is that I needed help from a higher power. Maybe some of you can face everything alone but I can also. It was my faith in God that allowed me to face my fears and understand more.

STEP 4: THE HEART CHAKRA: LOVE

The two forms of the soul (male and female) merge at the subtle form of the heart chakra. Some people are dominated by their thoughts and some are dominated by their feelings.

This conflict is faced in the heart chakra and one will dominate the other determined by many factors. Logic or feelings?

The next study is on cleansing the heart chakra. When the subtle of the soul combine, the heart chakra, throat chakra and mind chakra. When they combine they assert your thoughts and feelings.

Steps to clean the heart – look at the heart honestly. Do you find any hidden parts painful? Any buried? Then make a plan to finish unfinished business of the heart.

It's all common sense. Be sensible. The heart makes you blind to common sense. If you have any unfinished pain allow yourself to grieve, do not bury the pain. The heart requires single minded determination to go forward not backward. Past is past, let it go. Once you have crossed the bridge from physical into heart feelings. The motivation to keep living comes from the heart. Once the heart chakra is cleansed. The soul is on full spiritual level. Pure love brings pure thoughts and good wishes but heart requires courage. I stress it again, what is the point of hanging on to pain? Release it. Time has come on earth with a rush of time to end all past suffering and grief. There is no place to take these pains into the future. Leave it here so we can all move on. Time has run out. Leave it and be relieved. No court will hear your plea. Move on, leave it and be relieved. This is a spiritual war of past VS future and it is fought here in the present. In a war there are pains, wounds and casualties. In a time of peace we could nurture those wounds but there is no time now. We are in a spiritual war of leaving the past and moving into the future at lightning speed. Answer; find the love in your heart with faith.

STEP 5: THE THROAT CHAKRA

It balances the heart chakra and the mind chakra. The heart is love and faith, the mind sees the truth while the throat chakra represents trust and feels deception. The mind and heart are kept in balance through trust. "Tell me lies, tell me sweet little lies" all lies are first recognized and examined in this area. It represents the interaction with the entire world and all your relationships. You use speech to communicate make all understand, be happy and content. The throat chakra is the physical expression of our capacity to communicate and relate with all in our universe (and our world of relationships). If I have always wanted to please others to be accepted, to attract love, I will always say "yes" to everything. Hoping this will lead me to acceptance, love and happiness. When we are lonely we cannot see the wrong and right of yes and no. the ability to speak out and say no is a powerful truth learned through suffering. How can you trust yourself until you learn the lesson of 'No'? "Read my lips NO". `

You can see why the throat disease develops desperately trying to balance the account books of right and wrong of your relationships what if some of them never balance? Can't be balanced? There is no right, there is no wrong, only God's eternal song. Only God can make right that which has gone wrong. Only God can understand it all and can make sense of it all. When you try to balance your metabolism, you become slow, tired sluggish, sleepy, want to cry, cannot be motivated. Or you are anxious, agitated, lose weight, cannot stop, settle, cannot feel peace, we can never see a way out of the prison or trap of our own relationships. Then we need God's help. When you cannot balance logic and the heart, doubts become fear. There is disruption of life's pattern. The soul needs to dig deep into self-inspection. The soul needs it parents again.

THE MIND CHAKRA, THE THIRD EYE

It's magic is the third eye of our inner vision. It is the connection between your physical experiences of this world and your brain, your minds interpretation of this world. You are constantly balancing your mind's eye between your physical experience and your understanding of truth. I mean of course your personal acceptance of your own religious beliefs and accommodating all that your own every day experiences. The mind chakra, energy center, is extremely busy juggling so many inputs of feelings, thoughts, experiences into memory. The third eye, the mind chakra, has to interrogate all other inputs including inputs from the heart and solar plexus chakra (fears).

The mind must decide ultimately on the well-known theory "fight or flight". Does the situation warrant me standing my ground or flight to save my being? This is no ordinary signal station. Such pressure on the mind that it is no wonder that our society is now faced with an increasing health burden of people 'giving up' or taking suicide. The mind can no longer face to play its part. The mind represents the eye of the soul. It connects all the chakras, the body and the higher self. It is also called the third eye. It is now important to say 'as is your vision so is your world'. Your attitude to life, people, politics, religion and your world determines what you experience. Answer; Vision

The highest attitude to the world is 'everything that happens is for the good of all' and 'all will be the best for all'. The highest vision for the world is one of 'pure thoughts and god's wishes for all'.

THE SEVENTH CHAKRA

The seventh chakra is the highest chakra and is situated above the body. It is completely spiritual, the spiritual guide of light of the soul. This chakra is like a star and shines above all souls. It's colour is purple and is the colour of spiritual energy. It is the guide to the soul to its spiritual fulfillment and to its path, to the purpose of the soul's life. For those of us aware of our spiritual journey this chakra anchors us to our spiritual higher self or our higher truth. It is our guiding light, the sparkling star of truth. The guardian of the soul's journey and the souls rights guiding the soul home. When you can see the truth in a soul shining brightly, you know they are on the correct path. For those souls who desire and want the connection the guiding light can be connected to god, the father of souls, the truth.

I believe that connection can be there through the 7th chakra, the spiritual guiding light. The heart and mind need to desire that connection. The soul has the freedom of choice and I don't think the supreme soul God the father, ever interrupts free choice. He gave us free choice. It is our gift. This 7th chakra can still be our guiding light for souls who do not desire that connection with God but who have a deep connection with spiritual truth. The wiser the soul, the deeper the connection with truth, the more the soul starts sparkling. (Have you ever seen a soul sparkle with truth, because I have). The truthful soul dances the dance of spiritual happiness. Truth can guide you through a life of fulfillment and happiness. For the souls that wish it, the 7th chakra can anchor you to a soul connection with God the father. He can be your guiding light because the supreme soul, God the father is truth by nature. So the soul will sparkle with light when it is connected and following a true path and also if it allows God the father to lead it in life on a true path. The connection of soul and parent is so special, so loving, so important and so real it can make life's journey much more light, easy and happy no matter how difficult the life's lessons that have to be learnt. Our life's lessons are a part of destiny. If you have God's love, what else do you need?

THE LOST SOUL

As far as I can see, a soul becomes lost when the souls mind is deceived. It believes a lie to be truth. The third eye of the soul is the mind's eye. Its purpose is to see truth and light. As is your vision so is your world. This should determine a person's attitude, view of people and experience of life. The positive attitude comes from a true mind. Everything that happens will be for the good of all. If the seed is good the fruit will be good. The soul becomes lost when the third eye is closed to light and can no longer see any of these positive things. The mind can lead you astray with lies. The proof of the lies to the mind is that they don't bring light to the soul they bring darkness. In the dark the soul becomes lost and then the truth is lost. When the mind is dark it can be led back to the truth by the light of a higher being. By the light of truth and by God the father. The soul has the choice of seeing the following or denying. A lost soul is a sad sight. A soul with no love or happiness. It is each ones choice.

Get back on track. I'm all for religion, all for spirituality, and all for self-inspection, whatever it takes in a positive way to get back onto the path of self-development, self-learning and self-enlightenment.

Now that you have read my article, did the penny drop with any of you? Did any of you have any self-realisation about where your thoughts are going wrong? I claim this to be 7 steps to self-transformation. I have tried to explain why each one is just as important as another. The summary revolves around self-introspection. Check your thoughts that come from all seven areas (chakras) and where necessary change those thoughts. I'm not saying it's easy if those negative thoughts have been with you for life, I'm saying it's worth the effort to check all seven centers. Change all negative thoughts to positive and I promise you the outcome will be peace, happiness and contentment. What all souls desire more than life itself.

SUMMARY:

So the soul will sparkle with light when it is connected and following a true path and also if it allows god the father to lead it in life on a true path. The connection of soul and parent is so special, so loving, so important and so real it can make life's journey much more light easy and happy no matter how difficult the life's lessons that have to be learnt. Our life's lessons are part of destiny and our contract on learning our life's lessons are signed even before we take birth. In other words God cannot take away the hard lessons life has to offer as a part of our path in destiny but he can make the learning more friendly, easy, loving and more acceptable.

He can bring warmth and joy to a heart. Love to a heart that feels none elsewhere. Destiny cannot stop a soul from loving God its parent. How lucky is a soul loved by God? IF YOU HAVE GODS LOVE, WHAT ELSE DO YOU NEED?

If you do not want God's love for whatever reason, but you love and desire truth; as I already stated – "the truthful soul dances the dance of happiness". Your truth will be your guiding light and will take you home. Love and good wishes to all God's children who live in the truth and the light that will guide us all home.

The Soul, the Mind and Pain

*I THE SOUL AND MY PAIN. "THE WELL WISH SOUL".
ALL I CAN DO IS WATCH YOUR PAIN,
AND 'WISH YOU WELL'*

All we spiritual beings are souls. I play the part of a doctor in this world. Each soul is given its path and its lessons to learn. We must move forward as best as we can. Which is what this article is about, moving forward on your own spiritual path and how pain comes to you and must be confronted. I am a doctor. I am supposed to remove pain, there are many types of spiritual pain I cannot remove and so I say 'I just want to wish you well'. The soul is the spiritual entity that makes your body move around, live, think and feel. The soul is supplied with an active mind, a judgmental intellect and memories of all sorts. You could argue that a baby has no memories but I could argue with you the opposite. So why bother argue?

The body feels pain when it is physically hurt but what I wish to discuss is the pain the soul can feel and how this pain is felt. I argue that the soul can feel pain through any of its so called organs. The mind can give pain, the intellect can view pain and memories can be painful. The heart can not only feel pain, over reactive. Work out which type you are.

To start with, the common ways the soul feels pain are-
1) Through the mind
2) Through the intellect and the souls vision of the world
3) Through the heart and through its memories (e.g. Broken hearted)

To start with in this article I am talking about 'the mind' and its capacity to cause pain. After discussing the difficulties of the mind, we go onto discuss the blessings the mind can give you through prayer, meditation and the peace that comes from knowing your spiritual relationship with God and the souls home of peace.

WHY IS SUFFERING NECESSARY

The world needs a good wash and a good cleansing to get rid of everything bad and dirty. Start with self-healing to change the world. Start with thyself. Cleanse the mind's eye first. Trust in God and be blind, let God be your eyes and trust him. By letting God be your eyes you will see more truth and light than before.

THE MIND

"The eyes are a mirror to the soul". When we let God be our eyes we see the world through his eyes. The world is perfect and beautiful. It is the people who are awful, yet God sees them all as his own. The largest most powerful source of our own sorrow is our own mind. The mind is a powerful instrument. In India they say it is a wild horse as it runs in many directions. It deceives us of truth and brings us sorrow. We must learn not to be deceived by our own mind. It is not our friend, it is not helping. In general it is hurting us, deceiving us, causing us pain. Let it go, don't rely on it.

We must learn first to be deceived by Maya. Our mind is our closest friend and has the choice to either look and listen to God (light and truth) or turn and listen to Maya (lies and all things black). It cannot hear more than one at the same time and is easily deceived by Maya. Maya is like the snake from the story of Adam and Eve. It is cunning, persuasive, makes a good argument and cannot say one word of truth, your mind can be easily tricked. You must make the choice. You will know that something is wrong, but can't think of what. Maya will continue lying to you saying that it's your job making you angry or upset, it is your parents, your loved ones, friends, family, it can blame just about anything. You can then take all things out of the equation like quitting your job, moving town, you could do just about anything it would change nothing. You would still feel something is wrong and you still be letting Maya whisper in your ear.

The first step to is acknowledge that is Maya lying to you and the one causing all of thing. Take a moment to go somewhere quiet and look at yourself and have yoga. There is absolutely nothing wrong with you. You are a beautiful soul and deserve to be happy and loved. God loves you. You love back. If you see things from the right perspective everything changes. You can be happy, content, and find peace. Stop all bad emotions; whatever they may be (angry, sad, butter, numb).

If you have love for god in your hear then rely on that love in your heart to guide you, rely on God to talk to your heart. Let your mind run rampage, do its own thing and don't act on any bad thoughts it brings to you. The mind can and will deceive you. You do not really hate your family or anyone. Ignore it. Your heart will tell you the truth.

The mind filters out all the vibrations around you and all the input of frequencies you know (people you are close to). This is where telepathy was first described. This is how people can feel if there is something wrong with a loved one in a far off place. This is a gift while you can understand it. It is not a gift when it tortures you. Some people are totally insensitive to their minds whole some people are oversensitive and it hurts.

Learning how to use your mind as it was intended to be used is an art. In meditation you can learn to use your mind to bring peace and leave other inputs which is then good for you. Many people pursue meditation for this. there are a number of types of meditation using the mind as the instrument to train you to experience peace and they are all good if they work for you. In my training I think they counted eight types of mind training available, I say if it works for you it is good.

Stop thinking of your mind as your enemy, it is not only a part of you it completes you. Our minds are one of the most powerful tools in the world given the right to make choice. It is our best friend and links us not only to the rest of the world and God, but links us to our souls. Without it we would be lost. Minds are the ones that bring science, inventions, create art, allow us to feel joy, happiness, love, they are a thing of wonder and beauty. They create beauty. Of course they can also destroy it. But that is our choice. As I said before it is all about choice, perspective. This is YOUR choice and that's the bottom line. You choose to be positive or negative; you choose God or Maya; black or white.

One day this world will find its peace it so deserves. We sometimes forget that nothing can last forever, including suffering. At some point light will return. You can't control others actions if they want to attack you, but you can control your own. What they do is their business and what you do is yours. You can't blame others for your actions they are completely your own.

Religious minded souls are those who believe in the existence of God. Hopefully people can start to understand the role of God as the soul's mother and father. They can use this analogy to accept this relationship inter their own lives and also into their own religions. You don't need to be a nun or a priest to live a life in harmony with God, to love God, or believe in God. You don't need to live in a monetary. God takes us and loves us as we are and with our worldly lives. Of course he knows and accepts us with our all.

God exists beyond our physical realm and is not in a physical form, yet this does not stop him from understanding the complexities of our human existence and in no way hinders his capacity to understand our human and spiritual problems and to be our guide. He can accommodate many religious teachings with broadmindedness and a vision of world unity. He can and will accommodate so many as the one God.

There needs to be a place that people can focus their future and hopes on, not physically but spiritually. All spiritual people knew the soul has a home; a place of peace, a place of rest, a place of welcome comfort. It's called the souls home because that's where the spiritual parent of the soul is. The mother and the father of the soul. It's a place of rest and comfort. At the end of the day when people are anxious, worried, stressed, depressed. For example, when children play too hard they get tired and say "I want to go home now". Everyone has experienced this. This is the analogy. We souls are tired now, the desire calls for the mother and father, our spiritual parents.

They should remember that all souls come from and belong to, an abode of peace. A soul world filled with souls of course! It's a place of rest and comfort. It's where the supreme spiritual parent abides. The mother and father of the soul. It's the home of peace. At a time of anxiety and stress this is what people want to experience, the peace of knowing this is where 'I the soul' came from, this is where 'I the soul' will return to. It's ok, I can stay here for now and experience the peace of the home through meditation.

Almost all meditation practices, give experiences of the peace of the home.

Everyone is Australia is driven by agitated anxiety and fear. Anticipation and fear of present and future. Motivation of actions is distorted and peace less. The soul needed to learn the coming and going to its home to be just balanced, adjusted. All need to meditate or pray on the home of good of sweet silence and peace. The alternative is the world you see, unbalanced, deranged, irritated thoughts and confused actions. An unbalanced world filled with unbalanced people on the brink. The negativity of subtle things is just as grand as the world because each feeds off the other. Lust and desire feed off anger which feeds of greed and needs. Ultimately all feed off the self-centeredness allied with all selfishness to this physical world.

A person needs to view and experience themselves as a soul, spiritual being. The soul needs then to accept it has a mother and father. With trust and faith in God, the soul's spiritual home, you can come into and experience peace and love. It is so easy. Learn to meditate. When you learn to experience peace through your spiritual practice you become a well wisher. Able to share you satisfaction by wishing all well and positive futures.

Crying for Reality of Pure Love

In 1986 I experience the pure love of God touching and I cried and cried and cried. Two senior spiritual people looked at me and said to eachother, "why is she crying?" I didn't answer, one said to the other, "she is crying for she is happy", and they went about their business of being senior – meanwhile I kept crying.

That was 20 years ago and now I can see something of it. Some of us feel very deeply from our hearts, and they have very sensitive hearts. When they are hurt, even a bit, leaves a lasting impression of tears. An illusion of tears.

For some of us with very sensitive heart – No "BIT OF LOVE" will do – the love must be all and engulfing, completely forever and real love. How can it be the 'REALITY OF PURE LOVE'.

I believe in my heart as a soul that the only soul who can fulfill those qualifications and requirements is the Supreme Soul – God our Father – Supreme Spirit – Ocean of Love.

I believe HE is the only soul with that much love that he can fill that great hole left in our hearts after birth of mediocre relationships, poor relationships, sad relationships and even soul destroying relationships.

The supreme soul is an ocean of light and an ocean of pure love and bliss. He is here to heal souls at this time of sorrow on this earth's time (day) of sorrow. He is here to fill our hearts with soothing healing love and comfort when nothing else will do or work. No human relationship can fulfill this role of healer of hearts – comforter of hearts. We are the long lost and now found spiritual children of a spiritually loving parent – and it is at this exact time he has to come to love us and take away the pain of a multitude of births.

His love washes away the pain accumulated from many relationships. His love gives us a reason to bear pain, to be compassionate and love eachother.

His love gives us hope and a reason to keep going, keep loving – in a world that shows no love. His love is proof that it is really a war of good and evil. Love will always defeat (conquer) hate. Light will always fill darkness.

For those of you who cannot feel that love – look around you for proof. Everyone I meet has stories of pain, despair, hurt and unkindness. But so many give examples of souls that are sent to us to shine in God's love and light. These souls may be suffering terrible illnesses or misfortunes that seem to pass over their shoulders as if not touching them. And despite their terrible predicaments, they shine love and light and actually give love to their so called carers. They are there as the spiritual fathers living proof of pure love – THE REALITY OF PURE LOVE – in conditions where this seems impossible.

In other world they are LIVING MIRACLES or examples of the POWER OF LOVE TO CONQUER that which you cannot imagine.

They MAKE THE IMPOSSIBLE HAPPEN.

Through the power of God's love, through the power of the spiritual higher beings pure and unlimited love.

It has taken 20 years for my heart to slowly be healed. As if by some magical spiritual surgeon – not by any human hand, I mean it's like I had a heart surgery – I can feel again; that which was numb is no longer numb, that which felt no joy can see joy again – and feel it.

Many examples have been there to show me back to the path of feeling that love. HOW LUCKY AM I? God keeps sharing love with me and I try and share it with others.

As my daughter would say – You can be defeated by illusions or you can look for and see the truth.

www.ingramcontent.com/pod-product-compliance
Lightning Source LLC
Chambersburg PA
CBHW070942160426
43193CB00011B/1782